Charles Dickens'
A Christmas Carol

adapted for the stage by
Ronnie Meek

WordCrafts   **WordCrafts Theatrical Press**

CHARLES DICKENS' A CHRISTMAS CAROL
Copyright © 2012, Ronnie Meek

All Rights Reserved

CAUTION: Professionals and amateurs are hereby warned that performance of **Charles Dickens' A Christmas Carol** is subject to payment of a royalty. It is fully protected under the copyright laws of the United States of America, and of all countries covered by the International Copyright Union. All rights, including professional, amateur, motion picture, public reading, broadcast, and any other reproduction by means known or yet to be discovered are strictly reserved.

All rights are controlled exclusively by WordCrafts Theatrical Press, 912 East Lincoln Street, Tullahoma, Tennessee 37388. No performance of this play may be given without obtaining in advance the written permission of WordCrafts Theatrical Press, and paying the requisite fee.

SPECIAL NOTE

Anyone receiving permission to produce **Charles Dickens' A Christmas Carol** is required to give credit to the Author as the sole and exclusive Author of the Play on the title page of all programs distributed in connection with performances of the Play and in all instances in which the title of the Play appears for purposes of advertising, publicizing or otherwise exploiting the Play. The name of the Author must appear on a separate line, in which no other name appears, immediately beneath the title and in size of type equal to 50% of the size of the largest, most prominent letter used for the title of the Play. No person, firm or entity may receive credit larger or more prominent than that accorded the Author.

Charles Dickens' A Christmas Carol
Copyright © 2012
Ronnie Meek

Cover art - *"Applicants to a Casual Ward"* by Sir Samuel Luke Fildes
Public Domain

All rights reserved. No part of this book may be reproduced, stored in a retrieval system, or transmitted in any form or by any means – electronic, mechanical, photocopy, recording, or otherwise – without the prior written permission of the publisher. The only exception is brief quotations for review purposes.

Published by WordCrafts Theatrical Press
912 E. Lincoln St.
Tullahoma, TN 37388
www.wordcrafts.net

Charles Dickens'
A Christmas Carol

adapted for the stage
by

Ronnie Meek

Characters
In Order of Appearance

Narrator
Ebenezer Scrooge
Bob Cratchit
Fred
Man 1
Man 2
Boy 1
Marley
Ghost of Christmas Past
Boy Scrooge
Young Scrooge
Fan
Dick Wilkins
Fezziwig
Mrs. Fezziwig
Fiddler
Belle
Child 1
Child 2
Child 3
Father
Ghost of Christmas Present
Mrs. Cratchit
Martha Cratchit
Peter Cratchit
Belinda Cratchit
Nellie Cratchit
John Cratchit
Tiny Tim Cratchit
Fred's Wife
Guest 1
Lady 1
Lady 2

Jenny
Guest 2
Topper
Want
Ignorance
Ghost of Christmas Yet To Come
Businessman 1
Businessman 2
Businessman 3
Businessman 4
Businessman 5
Charwoman
Joe
Mrs. Dilber
Boy 2
Grocer
Housekeeper

Extras
Towns people, young men and women, boys and girls. These characters may be doubled from existing characters.

Charles Dickens'
A Christmas Carol

ACT I

Scene 1

SETTING: SCROOGE'S office.

AT RISE: SCROOGE is seated at his desk. BOB CRATCHIT is at his desk, eyeing the dying fire.

NARRATOR
Marley was dead. This must be distinctly understood, or nothing wonderful can come of the story I am going to relate. Scrooge knew he was dead? Of course he did. How could it be otherwise? Scrooge and he were partners for I don't know how many years. Scrooge was his sole executor, his sole administrator, his sole friend, and sole mourner. And even Scrooge was not so dreadfully cut up by the sad event, but that he was an excellent man of business on the very day of the funeral, and solemnized it with an undoubted bargain.

Scrooge! a squeezing, wrenching, grasping, scraping, clutching, covetous old sinner! Secret, and self-contained, and solitary as an oyster. The cold within him froze his old features, he carried his own low temperature always about with him; he iced his office in the dog-days; and didn't thaw it one degree at Christmas. Nobody ever stopped him in the street to say, "My dear Scrooge, how are you. When will you come to see me."

But what did Scrooge care! It was the very thing he liked, to edge his way along the crowded paths of life, warning all human sympathy to keep its distance. Once upon a time -- of all the good days in the year, on Christmas Eve -- old Scrooge sat busy in his counting-house.

>(Enter **FRED** who stops first to greet **BOB** then proceeds to his uncle's desk.)

FRED
Merry Christmas, Bob Cratchit!

BOB
Merry Christmas, sir.

FRED
How is that fine family of yours, Mr. Cratchit?

BOB
Well. They are all doing well. Thank you for remembering them, sir.

FRED
I'm glad to hear it. Be sure and remember me to them won't you.

BOB
I certainly will, sir.

FRED
Merry Christmas, Uncle!
>(**SCROOGE** does not respond.)
I said, "Merry Christmas, Uncle."

SCROOGE
Uh? So you did.

FRED
Ah, merry Christmas, uncle! God save you!

SCROOGE
Bah! Humbug!

FRED
Christmas a humbug, Uncle! I'm sure you don't mean that.

SCROOGE
I am sure I do. Merry Christmas! What right have you to be merry? What reason have you to be merry? You're poor enough.

FRED
Come then, what right have you to be dismal? What reason have you to be morose? You're rich enough.

SCROOGE
Bah! Humbug.

FRED
Don't be cross, Uncle.

SCROOGE
What else can I be when I live in such a world of fools as this Merry Christmas! What's Christmas time to you but a time for paying bills without money; a time for finding yourself a year older, but not an hour richer. If I could work my will every idiot who goes about with "Merry Christmas" on his lips, should be boiled with his own pudding, and buried with a stake of holly through his heart.

FRED
Uncle! Surely you don't mean that!

SCROOGE
With all my heart. You keep Christmas in your own way, and let me keep it in mine.

FRED
Keep it! But you don't keep it.

SCROOGE
Let me leave it alone, then! Much good may it do you. Much good it has ever done you!

FRED
There are many things from which I might have derived good, by which I have not profited, I dare say, Christmas among the rest. But I am sure I have always thought of Christmas time, when it has come round -- apart from the veneration due to its sacred name and origin, if anything belonging to it can be apart from that -- as a good time: a kind, forgiving, charitable, pleasant time: the only time I know of, in the long calendar of the year, when men and women seem by one consent to open their shut-up hearts freely, and to think of people below them as if they really were fellow-passengers to the grave, and not another race of creatures bound on other journeys. And therefore, Uncle, though it has never put a scrap of gold or silver in my pocket, I believe that it has done me good, and will do me good; and I say, "God bless it!"

(**BOB CRATCHIT** bursts into applause.)

SCROOGE
Let me hear another sound from you and you'll keep your Christmas by losing your situation.
(To **FRED**.)
You're quite a powerful speaker, sir. I wonder you don't go into Parliament.

FRED
Don't be angry, Uncle. Come! Dine with us to-morrow.

SCROOGE
I'll come see you in hell first.

FRED
But why? Why?

SCROOGE
Why did you get married?

FRED
Because I fell in love.

SCROOGE
Because you fell in love! Good afternoon!

FRED
Nay, Uncle, but you never came to see me before that happened. Why give it as a reason for not coming now? I want nothing from you; I ask nothing of you; why cannot we be friends?

SCROOGE
Good afternoon.

FRED
I am sorry, with all my heart, to find you so resolute. We have never had any quarrel, so far as I know. But I have made the trial in homage to Christmas, and I'll keep my Christmas humor to the last. So a Merry Christmas, Uncle!

SCROOGE
Good afternoon!

FRED
And a Happy New Year!

SCROOGE
Good afternoon!

FRED
Don't forget to mention me to the family, Mr. Cratchit.

BOB
Oh, I'll be sure and do so, Mr. Hollywell.

SCROOGE
There's another fellow, my clerk, with fifteen shillings a week, and a wife and family, talking about a merry Christmas. I'll retire to Bedlam.

(As **FRED** leaves **MAN 1** and **MAN 2** enter.)

MAN 1
(To **BOB CRATCHIT**.)
Good day, sir. We would like to speak to the owner, if you please.

BOB
Good day, gentlemen, right this way.
(He directs them to **SCROOGE**.)
There are some gentlemen here to see you, sir.

MAN 1
Scrooge and Marley's, I believe? Have I the pleasure of addressing Mr. Scrooge, or Mr. Marley?

SCROOGE
Mr. Marley has been dead these seven years. He died seven years ago, this very night.

MAN 1
We have no doubt his liberality is well represented by his surviving partner.

MAN 2
At this festive season of the year, Mr. Scrooge, it is more than usually desirable that we should make some slight provision for the Poor and destitute, who suffer greatly at the present time. Many thousands are in want of common necessaries; hundreds of thousands are in want of common comforts, sir.

SCROOGE
Are there no prisons?

MAN 2
Plenty of prisons.

SCROOGE
And the workhouses? Are they still in operation?

MAN 2
They are. Still, I wish I could say they were not.

SCROOGE
The Treadmill and the Poor Law are in full vigor, then?

MAN 2
Both very busy, sir.

SCROOGE
Oh! I was afraid, from what you said at first, that something had occurred to stop them in their useful course, I'm very glad to hear it.

MAN 1
Under the impression that they scarcely furnish Christian cheer of mind or body to the multitude, a few of us are endeavoring to

raise a fund to buy the Poor some meat and drink, and means of warmth. We choose this time, because it is a time, of all others, when Want is keenly felt, and Abundance rejoices.

MAN 2
What shall we put you down for?

SCROOGE
Nothing!

MAN 1
You wish to be anonymous?

SCROOGE
I wish to be left alone. Since you ask me what I wish, gentlemen, that is my answer. I don't make merry myself at Christmas and I can't afford to make idle people merry. I help to support the establishments I have mentioned: they cost enough: and those who are badly off must go there.

MAN 2
Many can't go there; and many would rather die.

SCROOGE
If they would rather die they had better do it, and decrease the surplus population. Besides - excuse me - I don't know that.

MAN 2
But you might know it!

SCROOGE
It's not my business. It's enough for a man to understand his own business, and not to interfere with other people's. Mine occupies me constantly. Good afternoon, gentlemen!

(**MAN 1** and **MAN 2** exit. Things return to normal for a moment when the door opens slowly and **BOY 1** steps in. **BOB CRATCHIT** smiles at him as he starts to sing.)

BOY 1
God rest ye, merry gentlemen. Let nothing you dismay...

SCROOGE
Here now! What do you think you are doing?

BOY 1
Singing, sir.

SCROOGE
Singing! Does this look like a performance hall?

BOY 1
It's Christmas Eve, sir.

SCROOGE
Oh, I see. You've come here to beg.

BOY 1
It's Christmas...

SCROOGE
Be gone, waif!
(**SCROOGE** reaches for his cane as **BOY 1** goes scrambling out the door.)
Christmas. Humbug! I wonder how many more beggars I'll be visited with this season.
(At this the bell tower strikes seven. **SCROOGE** stiffens in frustration as **BOB CRATCHIT** hastens to close up shop.)
You'll want all day tomorrow, I suppose?

BOB
If quite convenient, Sir.

SCROOGE
It's not convenient, and it's not fair. If I was to stop half-a-crown for it, you'd think yourself ill-used, I'll be bound? And yet, you don't think me ill-used, when I pay a day's wages for no work.

BOB
Christmas comes but once a year, Mr. Scrooge.

SCROOGE
A poor excuse for picking a man's pocket every twenty-fifth of December! But I suppose you must have the whole day. Be here all the earlier next morning, Cratchit!

BOB
Thank you, Mr. Scrooge! God bless you, sir... and... merry Christmas.

SCROOGE
Humbug!

(**BOB CRATCHIT** exits quickly before **SCROOGE** can change his mind.)

ACT I

Scene 2

SETTING: SCROOGE'S bedroom.

AT RISE: SCROOGE is sitting in his housecoat.

MARLEY (VO)
Scrooge!

SCROOGE
Marley? No, humbug.
(An old unused bell in the corner of the room starts to tinkle. He goes over to examine it.)
There must be a draft coming from somewhere.
(As he turns to go back the bell starts to ring violently soon joined by every bell in the house. The famous dragging of chains and slamming of doors happens starting in the cellar and quickly ascending toward **SCROOGE'S** room. Finally, **MARLEY** appears. The fire in the fireplace flares at his entrance.)
How now! What do you want with me?

MARLEY
Much!

SCROOGE
Who are you?

MARLEY
Ask me who I was.

SCROOGE
Who were you then? You're particular, for a shade.

MARLEY
In life I was your partner, Jacob Marley.

SCROOGE
Can you – can you sit down?'

MARLEY
I can.

SCROOGE
Do it, then.

MARLEY
You don't believe in me.

SCROOGE
I don't.

MARLEY
What evidence would you have of my reality beyond that of your senses?

SCROOGE
I don't know.

MARLEY
Why do you doubt your senses?

SCROOGE
Because, a little thing affects them. A slight disorder of the stomach makes them cheats. You may be an undigested bit of beef, a blot of mustard, a crumb of cheese, a fragment of an

underdone potato. There's more of gravy than of grave about you, whatever you are!

> (At this **MARLEY** raises a frightful cry, and shakes his chains.)

Mercy! Dreadful apparition, why do you trouble me?

MARLEY
Man of the worldly mind! Do you believe in me or not?

SCROOGE
I do, I must. But why do spirits walk the earth, and why do they come to me?

MARLEY
It is required of every man that the spirit within him should walk abroad among his fellow-men, and travel far and wide; and if that spirit goes not forth in life, it is condemned to do so after death -- and witness what it cannot share, but might have shared on earth, and turned to happiness!

SCROOGE
You are fettered, Jacob, tell me why?

MARLEY
I wear the chain I forged in life. I made it link by link, and yard by yard; I girded it on of my own free will, and of my own free will I wore it. Is its pattern strange to you? Or would you know the weight and length of the strong coil you bear yourself? It was full as heavy and as long as this, seven Christmas Eves ago. You have labored on it, since. It is a ponderous chain!

SCROOGE
Jacob, Old Jacob Marley, speak comfort to me, Jacob.

MARLEY
I have none to give. That comes from other regions, Ebenezer Scrooge, and is conveyed by other ministers, to other kinds of men. Nor can I tell you what I would. I cannot rest, I cannot stay, I cannot linger anywhere. In life my spirit never roved beyond the narrow limits of our money-changing hole; and weary journeys lie before me!

SCROOGE
You might have got over a great quantity of ground in seven years.

MARLEY
Oh! captive, bound, and double-ironed not to know that no space of regret can make amends for one life's opportunities misused! Yet such was I! Oh! such was I!

SCROOGE
But you were always a good man of business, Jacob.

MARLEY
Business! Mankind was my business. The common welfare was my business; charity, mercy, forbearance, and benevolence, were, all, my business. The dealings of my trade were but a drop of water in the comprehensive ocean of my business! Hear me! My time is nearly gone.

SCROOGE
I will, but don't be hard upon me, Jacob! Pray!

MARLEY
How it is that I appear before you in a shape that you can see, I may not tell. I have sat invisible beside you many and many a day. That is no light part of my penance. I am here to-night to warn you, that you have yet a chance and hope of escaping my fate. A chance and hope of my procuring, Ebenezer.

SCROOGE
You were always a good friend to me, Thank'ee!

MARLEY
You will be haunted by Three Spirits.

SCROOGE
Is that the chance and hope you mentioned, Jacob?

MARLEY
It is.

SCROOGE
Then - I think I'd rather not.

MARLEY
Without their visits you cannot hope to shun the path I tread. Expect the first to-morrow, when the bell tolls One.

SCROOGE
Couldn't I take 'em all at once, and have it over, Jacob?

MARLEY
Expect the second on the next night at the same hour. The third, more mercurial, will appear in his own good time. Look to see me no more; and look that, for your own sake, you remember what has passed between us.

(The lights dim and **MARLEY** vanishes. **SCROOGE** rushes to where **MARLEY** was and finds nothing. All is as it was.)

SCROOGE
Bah! Humb..."

ACT I

Scene 3

SETTING: SCROOGE'S bedroom.

AT RISE: SCROOGE is in his bed.

NARRATOR
SCROOGE could not bring himself to fully say the word "humbug." Of course it was humbug. There are no such things as ghosts. Unable to sleep, he told himself that he was simply not tired, but the truth was that he was not easy. Imagine his disconcertion when he was awakened by the neighborhood church bells sounding the four quarters followed by the striking of the hour with twelve bells. Twelve! It was past two when he went to bed. Twelve! He remembered that he had been warned of a visitation when the bell tolled One. So it was that SCROOGE was wide awake when next the clock struck the four quarters.

(**SCROOGE** counts as the clock bell rings.)

SCROOGE
A quarter past. Half past. A quarter to it. The hour itself. And nothing more. Well, Jacob Marley, where is this specter you spoke of, hmmm? Mistaken in death just as you were in life, old friend.
(**GHOST OF CHRISTMAS PAST** appears, startling **SCROOGE**.)
Are you the spirit whose coming was foretold to me?

GHOST OF CHRISTMAS PAST
I am.

SCROOGE
Who, and what, are you?

GHOST OF CHRISTMAS PAST
I am the Ghost of Christmas Past.

SCROOGE
Long past?

GHOST OF CHRISTMAS PAST
No. Your past.

SCROOGE
May I ask what business brings you to me?

GHOST OF CHRISTMAS PAST
Your welfare!

SCROOGE
Well, I am much obliged to be sure, but I can think of no greater benefit to my welfare than a night of unbroken rest.

GHOST OF CHRISTMAS PAST
Your reclamation, then. Be careful, Ebenezer! Rise! and fly with me!

SCROOGE
But I am mortal and liable to fall.

GHOST OF CHRISTMAS PAST
Bear but a touch of my hand and you shall be upheld in more than this!

(**SCROOGE** and the **GHOST** move together to an outdoor country scene.)

ACT I

Scene 4

SETTING: A countryside leading to the interior of a school house.

AT RISE: **SCROOGE** and **GHOST OF CHRISTMAS PAST** enter.

SCROOGE
Good Heaven! I know this place! I was bred in this place. I was a boy here!

GHOST OF CHRISTMAS PAST
You recollect the way?

SCROOGE
Remember it! I could walk it blindfold.

GHOST OF CHRISTMAS PAST
Strange to have forgotten it for so many years! Let us go on.

(Three **YOUNG BOYS** come running past.)

SCROOGE
I know them. They are my mates! Thomas! Thomas Figg! It's me! Ebenezer!

GHOST OF CHRISTMAS PAST
It's no good to call to them. These are but shadows of the things that have been. They have no consciousness of us.

(**SCROOGE** and the **GHOST** come to the interior of a school house. **BOY SCROOGE** is inside reading a book all alone.)

GHOST OF CHRISTMAS PAST

You remember this place of course. It is your old school. It is Christmas time now so everyone has gone home for the season. Well, not everyone is it? No, a solitary child, neglected by his friends, is left there still.

SCROOGE
Yes, spirit, I know the place well.

GHOST OF CHRISTMAS PAST
Pity that the poor boy has no friends with whom to share the season.

SCROOGE
Yes, well, his father was a difficult man and rarely sent for him even at Christmas. But you can spare me your pity. He's hardly alone. He has his books.

GHOST OF CHRISTMAS PAST
Of course! He has his books and all of those fascinating characters, but they aren't real.

SCROOGE
Not real! Ali Baba not real? And Robinson Crusoe, and Friday, and the Parrot, not real? He'll do alright, this one. You need shed no tears for him.

GHOST OF CHRISTMAS PAST
I wonder, who does shed tears for him? Robinson Crusoe? The Parrot?

SCROOGE
What?

> (**SCROOGE** is caught off guard by this remark. The **BOY SCROOGE**, obviously forlorn, shuts the book and leaves the room. **SCROOGE** is moved.)

I wish... but it's too late now.

GHOST OF CHRISTMAS PAST
What is the matter?

SCROOGE
Nothing. Nothing, there was a boy singing a Christmas Carol at my door last night. I should like to have given him something: that's all.

GHOST OF CHRISTMAS PAST
Let us see another Christmas!

> (**YOUNG SCROOGE** walks into the room. **FAN** enters.)

FAN
Ebenezer! Ebenezer! Dear, dear brother!

YOUNG SCROOGE
Fan! Sister! How wonderful to see you!

FAN
More wonderful than you know. I have come to bring you home, dear brother! To bring you home!

YOUNG SCROOGE
Home, Fan?

FAN
Yes! Home, for good and all. Home, for ever and ever. Father is so much kinder than he used to be, that home's like Heaven! He spoke so gently to me one dear night when I was going to bed, that I was not afraid to ask him once more if you might come home; and he said "Yes, you should;" and sent me in a coach to bring you. And you're to be a man! and are never to come back here; but first, we're to be together all the Christmas long, and have the merriest time in all the world.

YOUNG SCROOGE
You are quite a woman, Fan!

FAN
Come, Ebenezer, the carriage is waiting.

>(**FAN** and **YOUNG SCROOGE** exit and **SCROOGE** is obviously filled with joy at this memory.)

GHOST OF CHRISTMAS PAST
Fan. Always a delicate creature, whom a breath might have withered, but she had a large heart!

SCROOGE
So she had. You're right, I will not gainsay it, Spirit.

GHOST OF CHRISTMAS PAST
She died a woman, and had, as I think, children?

SCROOGE
One child.

GHOST OF CHRISTMAS PAST
Ah yes, your nephew! Fred Hollywell. He bears a great resemblance to her don't you think?

SCROOGE
I never noticed. But now that you mention it...

GHOST OF CHRISTMAS PAST
Come, Ebenezer, we must visit another Christmas.

ACT I

Scene 5

SETTING: FEZZIWIG'S warehouse.

AT RISE: YOUNG SCROOGE and DICK WILKINS look over the legers with FEZZIWIG.

GHOST OF CHRISTMAS PAST
Do you know this place?

SCROOGE
Know it! Why I was apprenticed here! Why, it's old Fezziwig! Bless his heart; it's Fezziwig alive again!

FEZZIWIG
Yo ho, there! Ebenezer! Dick!

SCROOGE
Dick Wilkins, to be sure! Bless me, yes. There he is.

FEZZIWIG
Yo ho, my boys! No more work to-night. Christmas Eve, Dick. Christmas, Ebenezer! Let's have the shutters up, before a man can say, Jack Robinson!
     (**DICK** and **YOUNG SCROOGE** clear things away.)
Hilli-ho! Clear away, my lads, and let's have lots of room here! Hilli-ho, Dick! Chirrup, Ebenezer!

(**MRS. FEZZIWIG** and her **DAUGHTERS** enter followed by an equal number of **YOUNG MEN**.)

SCROOGE
Why, it's Mrs. Fezziwig and her daughters followed by their young suitors!

FEZZIWIG
My dear! You look marvelous! All of you, my dears. What a blessed man I am.

(Guests enter, including a fiddler who takes his place for the music. The last to come in is **BELLE**. **YOUNG SCROOGE** has been looking for her. He can hardly take his eyes off of her. He is enchanted but shy. As he stands behind **BELLE**, **FEZZIWIG** sees his reticence and gives him a nudge into **BELLE**.)

BELLE
Oh! Oh, Ebenezer, it's you.

YOUNG SCROOGE
Good evening, Miss Belle. Please excuse me. Someone must have bumped into me.

BELLE
Really? And here I was thinking that you were trying to get my attention.

YOUNG SCROOGE
I was. I mean... no I... would you like something to drink, Miss Belle?

BELLE
Really, Mr. Scrooge, I am well prepared to share your company but I must insist that you brighten your countenance. It is Christmas after all and a smile would be in order.

YOUNG SCROOGE
I must warn you, Miss Belle, that I am of a serious disposition; however, in honor of your company I shall do my best.

FEZZIWIG
Here now, you two, it's time to dance. Belle, Ebenezer, there will be plenty of time to stand under the mistletoe later.

YOUNG SCROOGE
Mr. Fezziwig!

FEZZIWIG
Come on Ebenezer, I was young once. Now I am older and I can tell you for sure that fortunate is the man who finds the right wife to go through life with.

DICK
Come on everybody! They are playing Sir Roger de Coverley.

FEZZIWIG
One of my favorites! What a blessed man I am!

YOUNG SCROOGE
Miss Belle, would you do me the honor?

BELLE
Why, Mr. Scrooge, I do believe you are smiling.

>   (**BELLE** takes **YOUNG SCROOGE'S** arm and they join in as the dance begins. **SCROOGE** is clearly enjoying himself. The lights fade leaving

the **GHOST** and **SCROOGE** in a pool of light. In the dark we hear the voices of **DICK** and the other guests. "It was the greatest party ever." "A night never to be forgotten." "Three cheers for Fezziwig! Hip. hip...")

GHOST OF CHRISTMAS PAST
A small matter to make these silly folks so full of gratitude.

SCROOGE
Small!

GHOST OF CHRISTMAS PAST
Why! Is it not? He has spent but a few pounds of your mortal money: three or four perhaps. Is that so much that he deserves this praise?

SCROOGE
It isn't that, Spirit. He had the power to render us happy or unhappy; to make our service light or burdensome. Say that his power lies in words and looks; in things so slight and insignificant that it is impossible to add and count 'em up: what then? The happiness he gives, is quite as great as if it cost a... a fortune.

GHOST OF CHRISTMAS PAST
What is the matter?

SCROOGE
Nothing particular...

GHOST OF CHRISTMAS PAST
Something, I think?

SCROOGE
No. No. I should like to be able to say a word or two to my clerk

just now! That's all.

(**DICK** and **YOUNG SCROOGE** reappear.)

DICK
Are you in love, Ebenezer? With Miss Belle?

YOUNG SCROOGE
The thought had occurred to me.

DICK
Ha, she's too good for you.

YOUNG SCROOGE
I know, but some day... some day I'll make my fortune and then I'll deserve her.

(Lights fade on **DICK** and **YOUNG SCROOGE**.)

SCROOGE
That was unnecessary, Spirit.

GHOST OF CHRISTMAS PAST
On the contrary, it was quite necessary. You were in love once, Ebenezer, and you did make your fortune, but perhaps a fortune isn't what's required to "deserve" a woman like Belle. We have one more scene to visit.

(The lights come up on **BELLE** as she waits for an obviously late **YOUNG SCROOGE**.)

YOUNG SCROOGE
Ah, Belle, there you are. I'm sorry to be running late, but the opportunity rose for an excellent deal to be closed and I couldn't break away.

(**BELLE** seems to be crying.)
Belle, are you alright? Look, I know how you feel but I did say I was sorry.

BELLE
It matters little, to you, very little. Another idol has displaced me; and if it can cheer and comfort you in time to come, as I would have tried to do, I have no just cause to grieve.

YOUNG SCROOGE
What idol has displaced you?

BELLE
A golden one.

YOUNG SCROOGE
This is the even-handed dealing of the world!

BELLE
You fear the world too much. I have seen all of your nobler aspirations fall off one by one, until the master-passion, Gain, engrosses you. Have I not?

YOUNG SCROOGE
What then? Even if I have grown so much wiser, what then? I am not changed towards you. Am I?

BELLE
Our contract is an old one. It was made when we were both poor and content to be so. You are changed. When it was made, you were another man.

YOUNG SCROOGE
I was a boy.

BELLE
Your own feeling tells you that you were not what you are. I am. That which promised happiness when we were one in heart, is fraught with misery now that we are two. How often and how keenly I have thought of this, I will not say. It is enough that I have thought of it, and can release you.

YOUNG SCROOGE
Have I ever sought release?

BELLE
In words? No. Never.

YOUNG SCROOGE
In what, then?

BELLE
In a changed nature; in an altered spirit; in everything that made my love of any worth or value in your sight. If this had never been between us tell me, would you seek me out and try to win me now?
 (Pause.)
Ah, no!

YOUNG SCROOGE
You think not, then?

BELLE
Oh Ebenezer, how terribly telling is your non-answer. I would gladly think otherwise if I could. But if you were free to-day, can even I believe that you would choose a dower less girl? I release you with a full heart, for the love of him you once were. May you be happy in the life you have chosen!

 (**BELLE** exits. **YOUNG SCROOGE** waits a moment then also exits.)

SCROOGE
I almost went after her.

GHOST OF CHRISTMAS PAST
"Almost" counts for nothing in matters of the heart. Why didn't you go after her?

SCROOGE
I had managed to acquire a small sum of money. Belle wanted to marry right away but I decided to use it to lay the foundations for our financial security, which I have achieved I might add.

GHOST OF CHRISTMAS PAST
Ah!

SCROOGE
Spare me your sarcasm. I was doing this for both Belle and myself, but she chose not to share in my success, so we went our separate ways. And now it is time for us to go our separate ways. I must demand that you take me home.

GHOST OF CHRISTMAS PAST
My time does grow short but we have one more stop before we are done.

SCROOGE
No! I do not wish to see it!

GHOST OF CHRISTMAS PAST
You have no choice. You have told me what you have gained. Now I will show you what you have lost.

>   (An older **BELLE** enters surrounded by laughing excited **CHILDREN**. One of the **CHILDREN** shouts "Here he comes!" as their **FATHER** arrives loaded down with packages.)

CHILD 1
Father! Father, can we open our presents now?
(The others join in, "Yes! Yes, father, please!")

FATHER
Absolutely not! Presents on Christmas Morning as usual. You may; however, carry them into the house.

> (This hardly dampens the clamor and gaiety of the scene. The **CHILDREN** compare packages and make excited guesses about their contents as they exit.)

CHILD 2
Father, will there be a Christmas tree in the morning?

FATHER
You must wait till in the morning to find out, my dear. Hopefully Father Christmas will not forget us. Now hurry along.

CHILD 3
I love you, father. I'm so happy!

(All **CHILDREN** exit.)

BELLE
Well, will there be a Christmas tree this year, "Father Christmas?"

FATHER
Hum. I think there just might be. Ah, Belle, you look splendid!

BELLE
Thank you, my dear. How was your trip into town?

FATHER
It was successful. However, the excitement of London seems quite tame compared to the excitement of our parlor. Oh! I saw an old friend of yours this afternoon.

BELLE
Who was it?

FATHER
Guess!

BELLE
How can I? Tut, I don't know. Mr. Scrooge.

FATHER
Mr. Scrooge it was. I passed his office window; and as it was not shut up, and he had a candle inside, I could scarcely help seeing him. His partner lies upon the point of death, I hear; and there he sat alone. Quite alone in the world, I do believe.

BELLE
Poor Ebenezer, so sad. Quite alone.

> (Lights fade as they exit leaving **SCROOGE** and the **GHOST** alone.)

SCROOGE
Spirit! remove me from this place.

GHOST OF CHRISTMAS PAST
I told you these were shadows of the things that have been. That they are what they are, do not blame me!

> (**SCROOGE** sinks to his knees and cries out as the lights fade.)

SCROOGE
Remove me! I cannot bear it! Leave me! Take me back. Haunt me no longer!

FADE TO BLACK

ACT II

Scene 1

SETTING: SCROOGE'S bedroom.

AT RISE: SCROOGE is sitting up alertly in bed with all the curtains drawn back. The clock chimes the four quarters and the stroke of One. After a few tense moments he lays back down, then is hit by a blinding shaft of light

GHOST OF CHRISTMAS PRESENT (VO)
Scrooge! Ebenezer Scrooge!

(**SCROOGE** climbs out of bed and moves toward the source of the light.)

GHOST OF CHRISTMAS PRESENT
Come in! Come in. and know me better, man! I am the Ghost of Christmas Present. Look upon me! You have never seen the like of me before, have you?

SCROOGE
Never.

GHOST OF CHRISTMAS PRESENT
Have never walked forth with the younger members of my family born in these later years?

SCROOGE
I don't think I have. I am afraid I have not. Have you had many brothers, Spirit?

GHOST OF CHRISTMAS PRESENT
More than eighteen hundred.

SCROOGE
A tremendous family to provide for! Spirit, conduct me where you will. I went forth last night on compulsion, and I learnt a lesson which is working in me even now.

GHOST OF CHRISTMAS PRESENT
Touch my robe!

> (**SCROOGE** does so and suddenly the lights blaze to day. People are coming from everywhere with packages and foods. An open air market breaks out full of joyous buying and selling while carolers sing and children run merrily at play.)

SCROOGE
There certainly seems to be a great deal of excitement going on. Doesn't there?

GHOST OF CHRISTMAS PRESENT
What?

SCROOGE
I was remarking about the general gaiety of this scene. Everyone seems... happy.

GHOST OF CHRISTMAS PRESENT
They are!

> (Church bells chime and everyone scurries off as shops close leaving **SCROOGE** and the **GHOST** all alone.)

SCROOGE
Where have they all gone?

GHOST OF CHRISTMAS PRESENT
Didn't you hear them?

SCROOGE
Hear what?

GHOST OF CHRISTMAS PRESENT
The bells! The church bells.

SCROOGE
Church bells?

GHOST OF CHRISTMAS PRESENT
Are you deaf, dumb, and blind? It's Christmas Day! Church bells? Christ mass?

SCROOGE
They've gone to church then?

GHOST OF CHRISTMAS PRESENT
(As to a small child.)
They've gone to church.

SCROOGE
Spirit, it seems that even though the grocers are gone I can still smell delicious flavors. Is there some peculiar type of flavor that emanates from your torch?

GHOST OF CHRISTMAS PRESENT
Oh yes, there is.

SCROOGE
Would it apply to any kind of dinner on this day?

GHOST OF CHRISTMAS PRESENT
To any kindly given. To a poor one most.

SCROOGE
Why to a poor one most?

GHOST OF CHRISTMAS PRESENT
Because it needs it most. Here, I'll show you. Do you know this place?

SCROOGE
No, I can't say that I do.

GHOST OF CHRISTMAS PRESENT
Of course you wouldn't. It's the home of Bob Cratchit, your clerk. He has only worked for you... how many years has it been now?

SCROOGE
Uh...several.

GHOST OF CHRISTMAS PRESENT
several years.

SCROOGE
Well, he really doesn't do too badly on 15 bob a week.

GHOST OF CHRISTMAS PRESENT
Perhaps he does better than you know, Ebenezer. Let's go in.

SCROOGE
No! I mean, I wouldn't want to interrupt...

GHOST OF CHRISTMAS PRESENT
As with the ghost of Christmas past we shall be completely unnoticed to those we observe.

(As they enter the **GHOST** proclaims a blessing.)

GHOST OF CHRISTMAS PRESENT
May God bless all who reside here, and may the joy of His Holy Christ Child enfold each heart.

(Present are **MRS. CRATCHIT**, **BELINDA**, **PETER**, **NELLIE** and **JOHN**. They are busy with preparations for the dinner.)

MRS. CRATCHIT
What has ever got your precious father then. And your brother, Tiny Tim! And Martha warn't as late last Christmas Day by half-an-hour!

(**MARTHA** enters.)

MARTHA
Here's Martha, mother!

PETER
Hurrah! There's such a goose, Martha!

BELINDA
Yes! You must see it!

MRS. CRATCHIT
Why, bless your heart alive, my dear, how late you are!

MARTHA
We'd a deal of work to finish up last night, and had to clear away this morning, mother!

MRS. CRATCHIT
Well! Never mind so long as you are come. Sit ye down before

the fire, my dear, and have a warm, Lord bless ye!

JOHN
No, no! There's father coming.

BELINDA
Hide, Martha, hide!

(**MARTHA** hides as **BOB CRATCHIT** enters carrying **TINY TIM** and his crutch. He kisses **MRS. CRATCHIT** but notices that there is an unnatural silence in the room.)

BOB
Why, where's our Martha?

MRS. CRATCHIT
Not coming.

BOB
Not coming! Not coming upon Christmas Day!

(**MARTHA** emerges.)

MARTHA
Here I am, Father!

(They all laugh and join in the gaiety as **MARTHA** runs to hug **BOB**.)

PETER
Tim, you must see the goose.

JOHN
Yes, you must. It's enormous!

(The boys make a sling seat to carry **TIM** while the two younger girls lead the way.)

MRS. CRATCHIT
Martha, I think you had better go with them to be sure some of that goose is left for the meal.

MARTHA
Of course I will, Mother. It is so very good to be here with you all at home.

MRS. CRATCHIT
And how did little Tim behave in church today?

BOB
As good as gold, and better. Somehow he gets thoughtful, sitting by himself so much, and thinks the strangest things you ever heard. He told me, coming home, that he hoped the people saw him in the church, because he was a cripple, and it might be pleasant to them to remember upon Christmas Day, who made lame beggars walk, and blind men see.

NELLIE
Mother, I think the goose is ready.

(**MRS. CRATCHIT** retires to the kitchen while the children all come in to set the table and bring parts of the dinner.)

SCROOGE
Spirit, tell me if Tiny Tim will live.

GHOST OF CHRISTMAS PRESENT
I see a vacant seat in the poor chimney-corner, and a crutch without an owner, carefully preserved. If these shadows remain unaltered by the Future, the child will die.

SCROOGE
No, no, oh, no, kind Spirit, say he will be spared!

GHOST OF CHRISTMAS PRESENT
If these shadows remain unaltered by the Future, none other of my race, will find him here. But what then? If he be like to die, he had better do it, and decrease the surplus population.

SCROOGE
I see. You use my own words against me.

GHOST OF CHRISTMAS PRESENT
Yes. And in the future perhaps you will forbear that wicked cant until you have discovered What the surplus is, and Where it is. It may be, that in the sight of Heaven, you are more worthless and less fit to live than millions like this poor man's child.

>(The goose is brought in to thunderous applause. There is great eagerness to eat.)

BOB
Ahem, aren't we forgetting something?
>(They all bow their heads.)

Dear Lord, for the gift of Your Son the Christ, and for this wonderful bounty You have set before us this day, we give Thee thanks. Amen.

>(The lights fade on the family leaving **SCROOGE** and the **GHOST** in a pool of light.)

SCROOGE
Amen.

GHOST OF CHRISTMAS PRESENT
What?

SCROOGE
Nothing.

GHOST OF CHRISTMAS PRESENT
But I thought you said...

SCROOGE
No, it was nothing. It's a rather "small" bird.

GHOST OF CHRISTMAS PRESENT
It's all Bob Cratchit can afford!

>(The lights come back up as **MRS. CRATCHIT** is bringing in the pudding to great cheers. There is a moment of mock anxiety as **BOB** samples the first bite and pauses to consider his verdict.)

BOB
Magnificent, my dear. I believe this is your greatest success since you married me!

MRS. CRATCHIT
Nothing could top that, Bob.

JOHN
Hurrah for Mother!

SCROOGE
Well, Mrs. Cratchit's pudding was a success. Perhaps we should leave now?

GHOST OF CHRISTMAS PRESENT
No, there is yet one more bit of ceremony to which we should attend.

BOB
Attention! Attention everyone. I propose a toast. Mr. Scrooge! I'll give you Mr. Scrooge, the Founder of the Feast!

MRS. CRATCHIT
The Founder of the Feast indeed! I wish I had him here. I'd give him a piece of my mind to feast upon, and I hope he'd have a good appetite for it.

BOB
My dear, the children; Christmas Day.

MRS. CRATCHIT
It should be Christmas Day, I am sure, on which one drinks the health of such an odious, stingy, hard, unfeeling man as Mr. Scrooge. You know he is, Robert!

BOB
My dear, some charity. Christmas Day.

MRS. CRATCHIT
I'll drink his health for your sake and the Day's, not for his. Mr. Scrooge. Long life to him. A merry Christmas and a happy new year! He'll be very merry and very happy, I have no doubt!

> (They all repeat the name, one by one, as if it were some sort of punishment, except **BOB** who alone says it with any warmth.)

PETER
And a Merry Christmas to us all!

BOB
Yes, Peter. A Merry Christmas to us all. God bless us.

TIM
And God bless us everyone.

>(They laugh and drink the toast. The lights fade on the scene as the Cratchit family breaks into singing.)

SCROOGE
Well, Bob Cratchit's made a point he has. Without my keen sense of business to provide him with employment there would be no feast at all.

GHOST OF CHRISTMAS PRESENT
Is that all you have learned from observing this family?

SCROOGE
Well... no, but a man has to speak up in his own defense.

GHOST OF CHRISTMAS PRESENT
Does he?

ACT II

Scene 2

SETTING: FRED'S home.

AT RISE: A party is in progress. There is much laughter and merry-making.

SCROOGE
What is this place?

GHOST OF CHRISTMAS PRESENT
Oh, just a place. Dinner is already eaten, but we shall join in the after dinner festivities.

FRED
He said that Christmas was a humbug, as I live! He believed it too!

FRED'S WIFE
More shame for him, Fred!

GUEST 1
Fred, the way you describe your uncle I should very much like to meet him.

LADY 1
But not in a dark alley.

FRED
He's a comical old fellow, that's the truth: and not so pleasant as he might be. However, his offenses carry their own punishment, and I have nothing to say against him.

LADY 2
I'm sure he is very rich, Fred.

FRED'S WIFE
That's what he has always told me.

FRED
What of that, my dear! His wealth is of no use to him. He don't do any good with it. He doesn't make himself comfortable with it. He hasn't the satisfaction of thinking - ha, ha, ha! - that he is ever going to benefit us with it.

FRED'S WIFE
I have no patience with him.

JENNY
Nor do I!

GUEST 2
You don't know him!

JENNY
Nor do I wish to.

(A general discussion breaks out over whether or not one should wish to meet **FRED'S** uncle.)

FRED
Attend! Attend, everyone. I do have patience with him because I am sorry for him; I couldn't be angry with him if I tried. Who suffers by his ill whims? Himself, always. Here, he takes it into his head to dislike us, and he won't come and dine with us. What's the consequence? He don't lose much of a dinner.

GUEST 1
What! I think he loses a very good dinner.

(They all join in with praise of the dinner.)

FRED
Well! I'm very glad to hear it, because I haven't great faith in these young housekeepers. What do you say, Topper?

TOPPER
Oh, I rather like young housekeepers.

(**JENNY** gives him a shove and everyone laughs.)

FRED'S WIFE
Do go on, Fred. He never finishes what he begins to say. He is such a ridiculous fellow!

FRED
Quite right, my dear. I was only going to say that the consequence of his taking a dislike to us, and not making merry with us, is that he loses some pleasant moments, which could do him no harm. And I mean to give him the same chance every year, whether he likes it or not, for I pity him.

GUEST 1
Hear! Hear!

JENNY
I pity him, too.

GUEST 2
You? You don't even want to meet him.

JENNY
Well, I can still pity him, can't I?

GUEST 2
I'm... not sure...

>(A general discussion breaks out over whether one is allowed to pity someone they have no wish to meet.)

FRED
Well, he may rail at Christmas till he dies, but I think I shook him yesterday.
>(Mock "ooh's" and "ah's" arise to general laughter.)

Right then. Let's play a game!

TOPPER
Blind man's bluff!

FRED'S WIFE
No! The last time we played you were peeking and kept poor Jenny cornered behind the settee, touching her...

TOPPER
>(With mock indigence.)

I did no such...
>(Before he can finish he is drowned out by general agreement to the accusations.)

LADY 1
I know! Let's play "forfeits."

JENNY
How, When, and Where!

TOPPER
Yes and No.

FRED
Alright! Alright, everyone. We shall play them all, but let's start with "Yes and No." Now, who should go first.

FRED'S WIFE
You go first, Fred.

LADY 1
Yes, otherwise you will win every round.

FRED
Well, if you insist. Alright. I have something.

LADY 2
Is it a plant?

FRED
No.

GUEST 2
An animal?

FRED
Yes, it is an animal.

JENNY
A large animal?

FRED
Somewhat.

GUEST 1
That's not yes or no.

FRED
Quite right. Then "yes" it is large.

LADY 1
Does it belong to a herd or a flock?

TOPPER
That's two questions!

FRED
He's right. Those are two questions, but the answers are "no" and "no."

FRED'S WIFE
Can you eat it?

FRED
Oh my goodness, no!

GUEST 1
Is it fierce?

FRED
Very fierce.

LADY 2
Does it live in the forest?

FRED
No, it doesn't live in the forest.

LADY 1
Can one see it in the zoo?

FRED
I'm afraid not.

GUEST 2
Is it fierce?

(Pause as all look at him and snicker.)
What?

FRED
Oh, very fierce.

JENNY
Does it growl?

FRED
Indeed it does.

JENNY
I've got it, Fred! It's a bear!

FRED
No, Jenny, it's not a bear. Now you have lost and are out of this round.

JENNY
Not a bear?

TOPPER
My dear, it isn't in the zoo.

JENNY
Not all bears are in the zoo!

FRED'S WIFE
I have it, Fred. It's your uncle Scrooge.

(They all laugh.)

FRED
Right you are, my dear. It is my uncle Scrooge.

(Greater laughter still.)

JENNY
Well, I think I should get credit for a bear.
(Pause)
It's the same answer.

(Laughter.)

FRED
He has given us plenty of merriment, I am sure, and it would be ungrateful not to drink his health. Here is a glass of mulled wine ready to our hand at the moment; and I say, "Uncle Scrooge!"

ALL
Uncle Scrooge!

FRED
A Merry Christmas and a Happy New Year to the old man...bear, whatever he is! He wouldn't take it from me, but may he have it, nevertheless. Every year I intend to go to him and say, "Merry Christmas, Uncle."

TOPPER
And every year he will say...

ALL
Bah! Humbug!

(The lights fade on the scene as they all explode into laughter, until only **SCROOGE** and the **GHOST** are illuminated.)

SCROOGE
Spirit, wait! I do not wish to leave.

GHOST OF CHRISTMAS PRESENT
The laughter was at your expense, Ebenezer.

SCROOGE
I know... but the evening was young. The occasion was quite pleasant.

GHOST OF CHRISTMAS PRESENT
So it was; however, not all are so blessed, Ebenezer. My time grows short.

SCROOGE
Are spirits' lives so short?

GHOST OF CHRISTMAS PRESENT
My life upon this globe, is very brief. It ends tonight.

SCROOGE
Tonight!

GHOST OF CHRISTMAS PRESENT
Tonight at midnight. Hark! The time is drawing near.

SCROOGE
Forgive me if I am not justified in what I ask, but I see something strange, and not belonging to yourself, protruding from your skirts. Is it a foot or a claw!

GHOST OF CHRISTMAS PRESENT
It might be a claw, for the flesh there is upon it. Look here.
> (From the foldings of his robe, he brings two children, **WANT** and **IGNORANCE**; wretched, abject, frightful, hideous, miserable.)

Oh, Man! look here. Look, look, down here!

SCROOGE
Spirit! Are they yours?

GHOST OF CHRISTMAS PRESENT
They are Man's, and they cling to me, appealing from their fathers. This boy is Ignorance. This girl is Want. Beware them both, and all of their degree, but most of all beware this boy, for on his brow I see that written which is Doom, unless the writing be erased. Deny it! Slander those who tell it ye! And suffer its destiny.

SCROOGE
Have they no refuge or resource?

GHOST OF CHRISTMAS PRESENT
Are there no prisons? Are there no workhouses?

(The clock strikes the four quarters and twelve chimes. The light fades on the **GHOST** leaving **SCROOGE** alone.)

SCROOGE
No, Spirit! Don't leave me here! I do not like this place. I want to be taken back to my room. You can't leave me here. This isn't fair. Spirit! Spirit!

ACT II

Scene 3

SETTING: An empty stage.

AT RISE: The **GHOST OF CHRISTMAS YET TO COME** appears.

SCROOGE

I am in the presence of the Ghost of Christmas Yet To Come? You are about to show me shadows of the things that have not happened, but will happen in the time before us. Is that so, Spirit? Ghost of the Future! I fear you more than any specter I have seen. But as I know your purpose is to do me good, and as I hope to live to be another man from what I was, I am prepared to bear you company, and do it with a thankful heart. Why will you not speak to me? Lead on! Lead on! The night is waning fast, and it is precious time to me, I know. Lead on, Spirit!

(A light comes up on three **BUSINESSMEN** engaged in conversation.)

SCROOGE

Spirit, I know this place! It's the Exchange. I conduct business here.

BUSINESSMAN 1

I don't know much about it, either way. I only know he's dead.

BUSINESSMAN 2

When did he die?

BUSINESSMAN 3
Last night, I believe.

BUSINESSMAN 2
Why, what was the matter with him? I thought he'd never die.

BUSINESSMAN 1
God knows.

BUSINESSMAN 3
What has he done with his money?

BUSINESSMAN 2
I haven't heard.

BUSINESSMAN 1
Left it to his Company, perhaps. He hasn't left it to me. That's all I know.

(Laughter.)

BUSINESSMAN 3
It's likely to be a very cheap funeral for upon my life I don't know of anybody to go to it.

BUSINESSMAN 2
Suppose we make up a party and volunteer?

BUSINESSMAN 3
I don't mind going if a lunch is provided, but I must be fed, if I make one.

(Another laugh.)

BUSINESSMAN 1
Well, I am the most disinterested among you, after all, for I

never wear black gloves, and I never eat lunch. But I'll offer to go, if anybody else will. When I come to think of it, I'm not at all sure that I wasn't his most particular friend; for we used to stop and "speak" whenever we met.

>(General laughter as The **BUSINESSMEN** begin to exit.)

Bye, bye!

BUSINESSMAN 2
Cheers.

BUSINESSMAN 3
Cheers. And don't forget to let me know about the lunch.

>(They exit. Lights come up as two more **BUSINESSMEN** walk across the stage.)

BUSINESSMAN 4
Well! Old Scratch has got his own at last, hey?

BUSINESSMAN 5
So I am told.

BUSINESSMAN 4
Cold, isn't it?

BUSINESSMAN 5
Seasonable for Christmas time.

BUSINESSMAN 4
You're not a skater, I suppose?

BUSINESSMAN 5
No. No. Something else to think of.

>(They exit without another word.)

SCROOGE
Spirit, I know these men; excellent men of business, all. But I don't understand. Why was I privy to those conversations? Who were these gentlemen speaking of in such a cold unfeeling manner? And why is that gentleman standing in my accustomed place? I should be here at this hour! But wait! As I am resolved to be a changed man it may be that my general habits will be affected, may it not?
You're devilish hard to have a conversation with. Lead on, Spirit, and I trust that other scenes you have to show me will reveal the answers to my questions.

ACT II

Scene 4

SETTING: A shabby, disreputable pawn shop

AT RISE: The **CHARWOMAN** enters carrying a bundle as the **LAUNDRESS** enters from the other side, also carrying a bundle. They are none too pleased to see each other but after a few tense moments they are joined by **JOE**, the proprietor of the shop.

SCROOGE
Spirit! What is this place? I would have no business to transact in a place such as this.

CHARWOMAN
Let the charwoman alone to be the first! Let the laundress alone to be the second.

JOE
Come into the parlor. You were made free of it long ago, you know; and the other ain't no stranger. We're all suitable to our calling, we're well matched. Come into the parlor. Come into the parlor.

CHARWOMAN
What odds then! What odds, Mrs. Dilber? Every person has a right to take care of themselves. He always did!

MRS. DILBER
That's true, indeed! No man more so.

CHARWOMAN
Why then, don't stand staring as if you was afraid, woman; who's the wiser? We're not going to pick holes in each other's coats, I suppose?

MRS. DILBER
No, indeed! We should hope not.

CHARWOMAN
Very well, then! That's enough. Who's the worse for the loss of a few things like these? Not a dead man, I suppose.

MRS. DILBER
No, indeed!

CHARWOMAN
If he wanted to keep 'em after he was dead, the wicked old screw, why wasn't he more natural in his lifetime?

MRS. DILBER
It's the truest word that ever was spoke. It's a judgment on him.

CHARWOMAN
I wish it was a little heavier judgment, and it should have been, you may depend upon it, if I could have laid my hands on anything else. Open that bundle, old Joe, and let me know the value of it. Speak out plain. I'm not afraid to be the first, nor afraid for her to see it. We know pretty well that we were helping ourselves, before we met here, I believe. It's no sin. Open the bundle, Joe.

JOE
Now, you just wait your turn.

CHARWOMAN
But I was 'ere first!

JOE

She 'ad an appointment. Let's see... um... towels, silver teaspoons, a pair of sugar-tongs... One pound, four shillings. That's your account, and I wouldn't give another sixpence, if I was to be boiled for not doing it. Besides, I always gives too much to the ladies. It's a weakness of mine, and that's the way I ruin meself.

CHARWOMAN

And now undo my bundle, Joe.

JOE

What do you call this. Bed-curtains!

CHARWOMAN

Ah! Bed-curtains!

JOE

You don't mean to say you took them down, rings and all, with him lying there?

CHARWOMAN

Yes I do. Why not?

JOE

You were born to make your fortune, and you'll certainly do it.

CHARWOMAN

I certainly shan't hold my hand, when I can get anything in it by reaching it out, for the sake of such a man as He was, I promise you. Joe! don't drop oil upon his blankets, now.

JOE

His blankets?

CHARWOMAN
Whose else's do you think? He isn't likely to take cold without 'em, I dare say.

MRS. DILBER
Not where he's goin.'

JOE
I hope he didn't die of any thing catching? Eh?

CHARWOMAN
Don't you be afraid of that, I ain't so fond of his company that I'd loiter about him for such things, if he did. Ah! you may look through that shirt till your eyes ache; but you won't find a hole in it, nor a threadbare place. It's the best he had, and a fine one too. They'd have wasted it, if it hadn't been for me.

JOE
What do you call wasting of it?

CHARWOMAN
Putting it on him to be buried in, to be sure. Somebody was fool enough to do it, but I took it off again. If calico ain't good enough for such a purpose, it isn't good enough for anything. It's quite as becoming to the body. He can't look uglier than he did in that one.

(**JOE** removes a flannel bag and discovers that it contains money!)

JOE
This is the end of it, you see! He frightened every one away from him when he was alive, to profit us when he was dead!

(Great laughter as lights fade, leaving only **SCROOGE** and the **GHOST** illuminated.)

SCROOGE
Spirit, you show me cruel avarice and unseemly gaiety. Show me some tenderness, some depth of feeling connected with death.

> (Lights rise on the Cratchit home. **MRS. CRATCHIT** and the **CRATCHIT CHILDREN**, except **TINY TIM**, are seated around the fire. **PETER** is reading from the Bible.)

SCROOGE
Spirit, there must be some mistake. I've already been here. This is the home of Bob Cratchit, my clerk.

> (The **GHOST** indicates that they must enter.)

PETER
And he took a little child, and set him in the midst of them.

> (**PETER** sets the Bible aside as **MRS. CRATCHIT** seems to be crying.)

MRS. CRATCHIT
The color hurts my eyes. They're better now. It makes them weak by candle-light; and I wouldn't show weak eyes to your father when he comes home, for the world. It must be near his time.

JOHN
Past it rather, but I think he has walked a little slower than he used, these few last evenings, mother.

MRS. CRATCHIT
I have known him walk with -- I have known him walk with Tiny Tim upon his shoulder, very fast indeed.

BELINDA
And so have I. Often.

NELLIE
And so have I!

MRS. CRATCHIT
But he was very light to carry, and his father loved him so, that it was no trouble: no trouble. And there is your father at the door!

(**BOB** enters.)

BELINDA
Father! Father, you're home!

JOHN
It's so good to have you home, dear Father!

BOB
It's good to be home, my darlings.
(This expression of cheer requires obvious effort.)

MARTHA
I'll get your tea for you, Father.

BELINDA
Come, Father, and sit by the fire.

(She leads him to his seat and **NELLIE** sits on his knee.)

BOB
How sweet you all are, my dears. Oh, and look at your sewing! How much you've accomplished. I'm sure you'll be done long before Sunday.

MRS. CRATCHIT
You went today then, Robert?

BOB
Yes, my dear, I wish you could have gone. It would have done you good to see how green a place it is. But you'll see it often. I promised him that I would walk there on a Sunday. My little, little child! My little child!

NELLIE
Please don't cry, Father. You have us.

BOB
"Yes. Yes, of course you are right. I have you all, and what blessings you all are.

MARTHA
Here's your tea, Father.

BOB
Thank you, my dear. When I was in town today I ran into Mr. Fred Hollywell.

MRS. CRATCHIT
Mr. Scrooge's nephew?

BOB
That's correct. Anyway, the most extraordinary thing happened. He is a kind man and when he saw that I was looking a little down you know, he asked what had happened to cause me sorrow. When I told him he said, "I am heartily sorry for it, Mr. Cratchit, and heartily sorry for your good wife." By the bye, how he ever knew that, I don't know.

MRS. CRATCHIT
Knew what, my dear?

BOB
Why, that you were a good wife.

JOHN
Everybody knows that.

BOB
Very well observed, my boy. I hope they do. "Heartily sorry," he said, "for your good wife. If I can be of service to you in any way," he said, giving me his card, "that's where I live. Pray come to me."

MRS. CRATCHIT
I'm sure he's a good soul, Robert!

BOB
You would be surer of it, my dear, if you saw and spoke to him. I shouldn't be at all surprised, mark what I say, if he got Peter a better situation.

BELINDA
Only hear that, Peter.

MARTHA
And then Peter will be keeping company with some one, and setting up for himself.

PETER
Get along with you!

BOB
It's just as likely as not, one of these days; though there's plenty of time for that, my dear. But however and whenever we part from one another, I am sure we shall none of us forget poor Tiny Tim – shall we – or this first parting that there was among us?

CRATCHIT CHILDREN
        (ad lib)
Never, Father!

BOB
And I know, I know, my dears, that when we recollect how patient and how mild he was; although he was a little, little child; we shall not quarrel easily among ourselves, and forget poor Tiny Tim in doing it.

CRATCHIT CHILDREN
        (ad lib)
No, never, father!

BOB
I am a happy man. I am a truly happy man!

>   (Lights fade on the Cratchit home leaving only **SCROOGE** and the **GHOST** illuminated.)

SCROOGE
Specter, something informs me that our parting moment is at hand. I know it, but I know not how. Will you now show me what I shall be in days to come?

>   (Lights rise on a graveyard. There is one particular stone from which the **GHOST** will not be swayed as he directs **SCROOGE** toward it.)

SCROOGE
Before I draw nearer to that stone to which you point, answer me one question. Are these the shadows of the things that will be, or are they shadows of things that may be, only? Men's courses will foreshadow certain ends, but if the courses be departed from, the ends will change. Say it is thus with what you show me!

(**SCROOGE** creeps towards the stone and discovers his own name, *Ebenezer Scrooge*.)
No, Spirit! Oh no, no! Spirit! hear me! I am not the man I was. I will not be the man I must have been but for this intercourse. Why show me this, if I am past all hope? Assure me that I yet may change these shadows you have shown me, by an altered life! I will honor Christmas in my heart, and try to keep it all the year. I will live in the Past, the Present, and the Future. The Spirits of all Three shall strive within me. I will not shut out the lessons that they teach. Oh, tell me I may sponge away the writing on this stone!

FADE TO BLACK

ACT III

Scene 1

SETTING: SCROOGE'S bedroom.

AT RISE: SCROOGE is violently clinging to his bedpost as if it were the **GHOST OF CHRISTMAS YET TO COME.**

SCROOGE
Please! Please, I... I... I'm in my own room! I'm alive! Hurrah! I'm... I'm alive.
    (He hurries to his knees.)
Oh Jacob Marley! Heaven, and the Christmas Time be praised for this! I say it on my knees, old Jacob; on my knees!
    (He rises and looks around the room.)
The shadows of the things that would have been, may be dispelled. They will be. I know they will! – I don't know what to do! I am as light as a feather, I am as happy as an angel, I am as merry as a school-boy. I am as giddy as a drunken man. A merry Christmas to every-body! A happy New Year to all the world! Whoop! Hallo! – I don't know what day of the month it is! I don't know how long I've been among the Spirits. I don't know anything. I'm quite a baby. Never mind. I don't care. I'd rather be a baby.
    (**SCROOGE** opens the window and hears a chorus of Church bells.)

Oh, glorious. Glorious!

    (**BOY 2** enters. **SCROOGE** sees him and calls out.)

SCROOGE
Hallo here! What's today?

BOY 2
Eh?

SCROOGE
What's today, my fine fellow?

BOY 2
Today? Why, Christmas Day.

SCROOGE
It's Christmas Day! I haven't missed it. The Spirits have done it all in one night. Of course they can. They can do anything they like. Hallo, my fine fellow!

BOY 2
Hallo!

SCROOGE
Do you know the Poulterer's, in the next street but one, at the corner?

BOY 2
I should hope I did.

SCROOGE
An intelligent boy! A remarkable boy! Do you know whether they've sold the prize Turkey that was hanging up there? Not the little prize Turkey; the big one?

BOY 2
What, the one as big as me?

SCROOGE
What a delightful boy! It's a pleasure to talk to him. Yes, my buck!

BOY 2
It's hanging there now.

SCROOGE
Is it? Go and buy it.

BOY 2
Go on!

SCROOGE
No, no, I am in earnest. Go and buy it, and tell 'em to bring it here, that I may give them the direction where to take it. Come back with the man, and I'll give you a shilling. Come back with him in less than five minutes, and I'll give you half-a-crown!

(**BOY 2** exits at a run.)

SCROOGE
I'll send it to Bob Cratchit's! He shan't know who sends it. It's twice the size of Tiny Tim. Old Fezziwig never made such a joke as sending it to Bob's will be!

ACT III

Scene 2

SETTING: Outside of **SCROOGE'S** home.

AT RISE: **SCROOGE** waits. **BOY 2** enters, followed by the **GROCER**, carrying the turkey.

GROCER
Look here, boy, if this is some kind of prank I'll box your ears.

BOY 2
It's no prank. The man was right up there.

SCROOGE
Indeed, this fine young lad speaks the truth. How are you, my good man! Merry Christmas! Good Lord! What a turkey!

GROCER
This 'ere's the prize turkey.

SCROOGE
I should say so! Here is the address to which it is to be delivered. But wait! There is no way you can carry that huge bird all the way to Camden Town. Here is money for a cab. It must be delivered in time for Christmas dinner.

GROCER
Who shall I say it is from?

SCROOGE
Anonymous.

GROCER
Anonymous? Oh, I get it. You don't want them to know who sent it.

SCROOGE
Right you are my fine fellow. Now be off. Oh, and here's a little something extra for your trouble.

GROCER
Thank you, sir. God bless you, sir.
(Exits.)

SCROOGE
And for you my fine lad... a half crown!

BOY 2
Wow! Merry Christmas, mister!
(Exits.)

SCROOGE
Splendid boy! Wonderful boy!

(The **GENTLEMEN** who visited the office the day before pass by. They tip their hats but appear not to recognize **SCROOGE**. He is brought short by remembering who they are.)

SCROOGE
My dear sirs, how do you do? I do hope you succeeded yesterday. It was very kind of you. A merry Christmas to you!

MAN 1
Mr. Scrooge?

SCROOGE
Yes, that is my name, and I fear it may not be pleasant to you.

Allow me to ask your pardon. And will you have the goodness…

(**SCROOGE** whispers in his ear. He in turn whispers to the other.)

MAN 2
Lord bless me! My dear Mr. Scrooge, are you serious?

SCROOGE
If you please, and not a farthing less. A great many back-payments are included in that figure, I assure you. Will you do me that favor?

MAN 1
My dear sir, I don't know what to say to such munificence.

SCROOGE
Don't say anything. Come and see me. Will you come and see me?

MAN 1
I will! We both will.

SCROOGE
Thank 'ee. I am much obliged to you. I thank you fifty times. Bless you!

ACT III

Scene 3

SETTING: FRED'S home.

AT RISE: SCROOGE knocks at the door and is greeted by the housekeeper.

SCROOGE
Is your master at home, my dear?

HOUSEKEEPER
Yes, sir.

SCROOGE
Where is he, my love?

HOUSEKEEPER
He's in the sitting-room, sir, along with the mistress. I'll announce you, if you please.

SCROOGE
Thank 'ee. He knows me. Fred!

FRED
Why bless my soul! Uncle Scrooge! What? What are you...

SCROOGE
Are you trying to ask me what I'm doing here?

FRED
Well, yes. What are you doing here?

SCROOGE
I've come to apologize for my behavior yesterday.

FRED
You have!

SCROOGE
Yes, Fred. Those things I said about Christmas being a humbug. I was terribly wrong. I didn't understand it then but I do now. Also, my rather rude reply to your generous invitation to dine with you today – that was very wrong of me. And if you could find it in your heart to keep the invitation in force...

FRED
"If" I could? Well of course it's in force.

SCROOGE
Your generosity of spirit humbles me, Fred. And yes, I would be delighted to dine with you and your friends today.

FRED
Hurrah! I knew that someday you would come around.

SCROOGE
You knew did you? Well, apparently you were right.

FRED
My dear! Go and have the housekeeper set another place at the table. But wait! How thoughtless of me. Uncle Scrooge, this is my...

SCROOGE
Don't tell me. This must be your lovely bride. Enchanted, my dear. My nephew has certainly done very well for himself.

FRED'S WIFE
Thank you. I'm flattered, Mr. Scrooge.

SCROOGE
Uncle Ebenezer, if you don't mind.

FRED'S WIFE
Of course, Uncle Ebenezer.

SCROOGE
I was in love myself once. Would you believe that?

FRED'S WIFE
Why, yes. Yes, I would.

FRED
Oh Uncle, you have made us so happy.

SCROOGE
Have I? Well, I've wasted many years, Fred. But I don't intend to waste any more. So, let's not waste a minute! Why don't we sample some of the Christmas bowl?

FRED
Excellent suggestion!

SCROOGE
Perhaps after dinner we can play some games?

FRED'S WIFE
Oh yes! Do you like games, Uncle Ebenezer?

SCROOGE
Very much. I enjoy word games and "Blind Man's Bluff."

FRED'S WIFE
One of our favorites.

SCROOGE
Ah, but will your sister be willing to play with Mr. Topper in the group?

FRED'S WIFE
(Laughs.)
You're right. I don't know if she will.

FRED
Uncle, how do you know...?

SCROOGE
Oh, I do get around, Fred. I do get around.
(Pause.)
Merry Christmas to you both.

FRED
Merry Christmas, Uncle. May God bless us all.

ACT III

Scene 4

SETTING: SCROOGE'S office.

AT RISE: SCROOGE waits for BOB to arrive.

SCROOGE
Late again, eh Cratchit? We'll see about this.

>(**BOB** comes rushing in. He goes straight to his stool and starts to work.)

SCROOGE
Mr. Cratchit! What do you mean by coming here at this time of day?

BOB
I am very sorry, sir, I am behind my time.

SCROOGE
Yes. I think you are. Step this way, if you please.

BOB
It's only once a year, sir, it shall not be repeated. I was making rather merry yesterday, sir.

SCROOGE
Now, I'll tell you what, my friend, I am not going to stand this sort of thing any longer. And therefore... and therefore I am about to raise your salary!

>(He tosses a small money bag into **BOB'S** hands. **BOB** is speechless.)

A merry Christmas, Bob Cratchit! And a merrier Christmas, my good fellow, than I have given you for many a year! I'll raise your salary, and I'm going to endeavor to assist your struggling family. Well, we will discuss your affairs this very afternoon, over a Christmas bowl of smoking bishop, Bob!

BOB
Thank you, sir.

SCROOGE
Well, what are you standing there for? Make up the fires, and buy another coal-scuttle before you dot another "i," Bob Cratchit.

NARRATOR
> (During this narration **BOB** runs out to buy coal and **SCROOGE** strolls out of the office to be met by a running **TINY TIM** who has no more need of a crutch.)

Scrooge was better than his word. He did it all, and infinitely more; and to Tiny Tim, who did not die, he was a second father. He became as good a friend, as good a master, and as good a man, as the good old city knew, or any other good old city, town, or borough, in the good old world. Ever afterwards it was always said of him, that he knew how to keep Christmas well, if any man alive possessed the knowledge. May that be truly said of us, and all of us! And so, as Tiny Tim observed, God Bless Us, Every One!

CURTAIN

www.ingramcontent.com/pod-product-compliance
Lightning Source LLC
Chambersburg PA
CBHW071411290426
44108CB00014B/1783